COUNTRIES OF THE WORLD

THE NETHERLANDS

Christine Osborne

with photographs by Christine Osborne

Illustrated by Peter Bull

The Bookwright Press
New York • 1990

Titles in this series

Australia	Italy
Canada	Japan
The Caribbean	The Netherlands
China	New Zealand
France	Pakistan
Great Britain	Spain
Greece	The United States
India	West Germany

Cover Porters at the weekly cheese market in Alkmaar.

Opposite A child being carried on its parent's bicycle is a common sight in the Netherlands.

First published in the United States by
The Bookwright Press
387 Park Avenue South
New York NY 10016

First published in 1989 by
Wayland (Publishers) Ltd,
61 Western Road, Hove,
East Sussex, BN3 1JD, England

Library of Congress Cataloging-in-Publication Data
Osborne, Christine.
  The Netherlands / by Christine Osborne; [with photographs by Christine Osborne; illustrated by Peter Bull].
    p. cm. – (Countries of the world)
  Includes bibliographical references.
  Summary: Introduces the history, family life, geography, government, economy, and education of the Netherlands.
  ISBN 0–531–18336–X
  1. Netherlands – Juvenile literature. [1. Netherlands.]
1. Bull, Peter (Peter T.), ill. II. Title. III. Series:
Countries of the world (New York, N.Y.)   89–17760
DJ18.078 1990   CIP
949.2–dc20   AC

Typeset by Rachel Gibbs, Wayland
Printed in Italy by G.Canale and C.S.p.A., Turin

Contents

Words that appear in **bold** in the text are explained in the glossary on page 46.

THE NETHERLANDS

1 Introduction

Netherland's place in Europe

Sweden
Denmark
Ireland
United Kingdom
Netherlands
East Germany
Poland
Belgium
Lux.
West Germany
Czechoslovakia
France
Switzerland
Austria
Hungary
Portugal
Spain
Italy
Yugoslavia
Albania
Greece

WEST FRISIAN ISLANDS

WADDEN SEA

Ems

GRONINGEN
Leeuwarden
Groningen

FRIESLAND

DRENTHE

NORTH HOLLAND

N E T H E R L A N D S

Lelystad
Zwolle

NORTH SEA

Haarlem
FLEVOLAND
OVERIJSSEL
Amsterdam

Apeldoorn
Enschede

Leiden
Utrecht
GELDERLAND

The Hague
(S'-Gravenhage)
SOUTH HOLLAND
UTRECHT
Lek
Arnhem

Rotterdam
Waal
Nijmegen
Dordrecht
Maas

ZEELAND
WEST GERMANY

Breda
NORTH BRABANT
Vlissingen
Tilburg

Eindhoven
SCHELDE ESTUARY

BELGIUM
LIMBURG

N

Maastricht

Major roads	Car Ferry
Major airports	Provincial borders
Major ports	

km 0 — 20 — 40 — 60 — 80
miles 0 — 10 — 20 — 30 — 40 — 50

The Netherlands is a **maritime** nation. The North Sea borders the west coast, and West Germany lies to the east and Belgium to the south of the country. Most of the country is low and flat, and throughout history the Dutch have had to battle against the sea. **Dikes** were built to hold back the sea as early as the seventh century AD. In the sixteenth century, **windmills** were used to drain water from the marshland so that it could be used for farming. There were once more than a thousand windmills, but today, although many are still to be seen, only a fraction are in working order. They have been replaced by modern pumps. Weather-watching is a serious business in the Netherlands. Any break in the dikes or the flood barriers protecting the country can mean tragedy. In 1953, disastrous floods claimed 1,835 lives in the southwestern province of Zeeland.

The Netherlands has made use of its geographical position and its network of rivers and canals to become a successful trading nation. By the seventeenth century it had **colonies** as far away as Indonesia and the Caribbean. Today, Rotterdam, at the mouths of the Rhine and Maas rivers, is one of the busiest ports in the world. The Netherlands has had economic and trading links with neighboring Belgium and Luxembourg for many years and the three are now known as the Benelux countries. Their main trading partners are West Germany, Britain and France.

The twelve provinces of the Netherlands contain many contrasts in terms of scenery, architecture and culture. Although small in area and population, the country plays a very important part in the **European Economic Community (EEC)**, of which it is a founder member. It is recognized as one of the most progressive countries in northwest Europe.

Windmills are still a common sight.

2 Land and climate

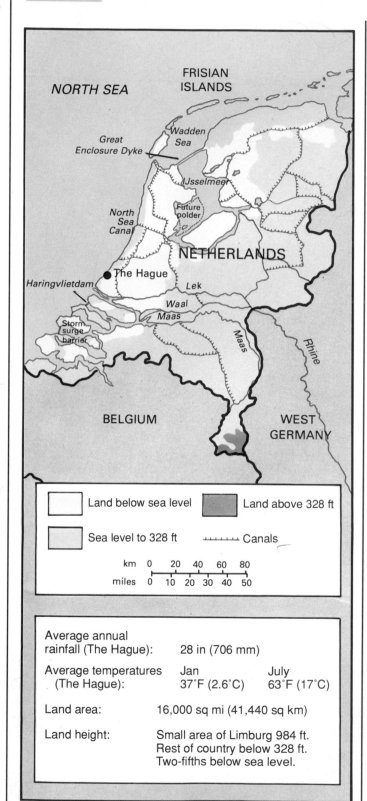

Land below sea level

Land above 328 ft

Sea level to 328 ft

++++++ Canals

| km | 0 | 20 | 40 | 60 | 80 |
| miles | 0 | 10 | 20 | 30 | 40 | 50 |

Average annual rainfall (The Hague):	28 in (706 mm)	
Average temperatures (The Hague):	Jan 37°F (2.6°C)	July 63°F (17°C)
Land area:	16,000 sq mi (41,440 sq km)	
Land height:	Small area of Limburg 984 ft. Rest of country below 328 ft. Two-fifths below sea level.	

Nederland, the official name of the Netherlands in Dutch, means "low land." This is a very good description. The country covers about 16,000 sq mi (41,440 sq km), but its average height is barely 40 ft (12 m) above sea level. Much of the Netherlands is actually below sea level and is protected from flooding by a system of dikes, dams, **locks** and **canals**. The only hilly area is the southern province of Limburg.

Wide, sandy beaches and dunes stretch from the Frisian Islands in the north to the estuary of the Schelde River in the south. The small lakes within the dunes, and the Wadden Sea between the Frisian Islands and the mainland, are a paradise for many different water birds.

This partly drained land, behind a dike holding back the IJsselmeer, is home to many water birds.

Above *The Great Enclosure Dike provides a fast road across the IJsselmeer.*

Left *Part of the Delta storm-surge barrier, completed in 1978 and made up of 65 separate steel gates.*

Today, approximately two-fifths of the Netherlands is land that has been reclaimed from the sea. The greatest achievement has been the draining of the inland sea – the Zuider Zee – which was started in 1919 and continues today. To separate it from the North Sea, a 19-mi (30-km) barrier, the Great Enclosure Dike, was built over the water between North Holland and Friesland. As the IJssel River continued to flow into the basin, it slowly turned into a freshwater lake. This was renamed IJsselmeer (meer meaning lake). New land, or **polder**, has been created by pumping areas dry. The largest polder, Flevoland, became the Netherlands' twelfth province in 1986.

Following the 1953 floods, the **Delta project** was devised to protect the low-lying areas of Zeeland. Now, huge storm-surge barriers can be lowered if floods are expected.

The Netherlands has a temperate climate with cool, showery summers and fairly mild winters. It is often windy, as there is no protection from the southwesterly winds that blow across the flat landscape from the sea. Occasionally, the winds are strong enough for the great Zeeland Bridge over the Schelde **estuary** to be closed. During the winter, sea mist and fog may hang over the marshes, and a cold spell may freeze the canals, making them very popular for skating.

3 History

Dutch Protestants were ruthlessly persecuted by the Duke of Alva, who acted for Philip II.

The country we know as the Netherlands has a history of wars and peace agreements stretching back for centuries.

Two thousand years ago early settlers built their homes on mounds of earth called *terpen*, which they raised to make them safe from floods. One thousand years ago, the area was being fought over by the Frankish people (who originally came from Germany). Norsemen were making raids from the sea and were also settling where they could.

The main towns of the Netherlands at that time – Ghent, Bruges, Amsterdam and Rotterdam – grew up from the twelfth century onward. They were known as "charter towns" after the agreements drawn up between the townspeople and the local lords, setting down rules for taxation, laws and military service.

In the fifteenth century, much of the country came under the control of Duke Philip of Burgundy, and his successors. One of them, Charles, also became King of Spain and Holy Roman Emperor in the first half of the sixteenth century.

During this time, many of the people of the Netherlands turned away from the **Catholic** religion and became **Protestants**. They were persecuted for this by those in authority, who imprisoned and tortured them to try to force them to give up their new religion. When

Philip II of Spain came to power in 1555, the persecution increased and the people rebelled, choosing Prince William of Orange as their leader.

For much of the next ninety years, parts of the Netherlands were at war with Spain. During this time, the northern provinces gained some independence and, with the Union of Utrecht in 1579, formed the United Provinces. This was the beginning of the modern state of the Netherlands, which we often call Holland, after the largest province.

Right Charles V, King of Spain and Holy Roman Emperor, who ruled the Netherlands from 1506–55. This famous portrait by Van Dyck was painted in the seventeenth century.

Below During the war against the Spanish, the armies of the United Provinces made many sea-borne attacks.

A typical scene in a Dutch town in the early nineteenth century.

Even though the United Provinces were still at war with Spain, they sent out ships around the world to find new lands and people with whom they could trade. In 1602 the East Indies Company was founded to regulate and protect trade with the Far East. Silks and spices were brought back, and colonies were established in Malaya and Ceylon. The West Indies Company regulated trade with North and South America and Africa. Both companies had their own armies and were given the right to wage war and sign treaties.

The United Provinces came to an end in 1795 when the country was invaded by the French, who ruled it until they were defeated in 1814. The Netherlands was then declared a united kingdom, and their leader pronounced King William I. To begin with, the kingdom included what had been the southern Netherlands, but these provinces broke away to form Belgium.

The Netherlands remained at peace for over one hundred years, declaring itself neutral during World War I (1914–18). But in 1940, Hitler invaded the country. Many of the Dutch joined the secret **Resistance** movement to fight the Nazis, and over 23,000 members lost their lives. The country remained under occupation for nearly five years, during which time people endured great hardship, particularly in the winter of 1944–5, when thousands of people died of starvation.

Since World War II, the Dutch have rebuilt their cities and factories, and are now a prosperous country once again.

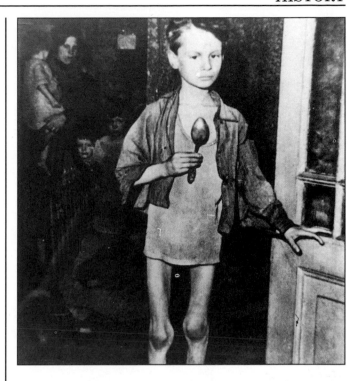

A starving Dutch child in the winter of 1944–5.

Important dates

1419	Philip of Burgundy acquires much of the Netherlands.
1550	Edict of Blood decrees death to all Protestants.
1555-79	Revolt of the Netherlands under Prince William of Orange.
1579	Union of Arras in which southern provinces agree to Spanish Catholic rule.
1579	Union of Utrecht in which northern provinces unite against Spain.
1602	Dutch East Indies Company founded.
1648	Treaty of Münster with Spain recognizes independence of United Provinces.
1652	First Dutch settlers colonize Cape of Good Hope, South Africa.
1652-4	First English War.
1664-7	Second English War (Battle of Medway).
1688	Prince William becomes joint ruler of England with wife Mary.
1798-1813	French occupation.
1815	United Kingdom of the Netherlands established under King William I.
1839	The Netherlands acknowledges Belgian independence.
1940	German invasion.
1945	Liberation of the Netherlands from German occupation.
1948	The Benelux Customs Union between Belgium, the Netherlands and Luxembourg comes into effect.
1954	The Netherlands joins NATO.
1958	Benelux becomes economic union. The Netherlands helps found the European Economic Community (EEC).

4 People and language

A woman in Dutch costume in a room decorated in traditional style.

The population of the Netherlands is 14.8 million. It is one of the most densely populated countries in the world, with an average of 1032 people per sq mi (400 per sq km). The Dutch are a polite, friendly, hardworking and home-loving nation. Family life is very important and, in general, the Dutch people prefer entertaining at home to eating in a restaurant. Their homes and gardens are well cared for, and nearly every windowsill holds potted plants or a window box full of flowers.

The Dutch are also said to be a tolerant nation. Over the centuries they have learned to live peacefully with people of other nationalities, both at home and abroad. In recent years the Netherlands, like Britain and France, has received thousands of **immigrants** from its former colonies. The largest group, numbering about 300,000, has come from Indonesia, many from the Moluccas (formerly called the "Spice Islands"). About the same number have come from Suriname and the Netherlands Antilles in the Caribbean. Other immigrants include people from Mediterranean countries, especially Morocco and Tunisia, who have moved to the Netherlands in search of work. Many have settled in the towns of Randstad Holland and in the Bijlmeermeer, the vast housing complex about a half-hour's train ride from Amsterdam. The influence of these immigrants is noticeable, especially in the new stores and restaurants selling food from all over the world.

The main language in the Netherlands is Dutch, although most young people today speak at least two languages. Many Dutch people speak English very well, and in the south some also speak French and German. In Friesland the old Frisian language can still be heard. Recent immigrants often retain their own language, but their children soon pick up Dutch from watching television and from classes at school.

Above A woman selling different kinds of olives imported from Mediterranean countries.

Right Moroccan farm workers relaxing in a café.

5 Amsterdam

Amsterdam, the capital of the Netherlands and the largest freshwater port in Europe, is very popular with tourists from all over the world. Reminders of the seventeenth and eighteenth centuries are seen along its canals: there are elegant houses, stately museums and splendid churches. Amsterdam can easily be explored on foot or by bicycle, and there are also bright yellow trams, buses and a subway system. Besides the old-world charm are signs of the modern age: automatic vending machines sell everything from tulips to French fries, and there are government-approved "Bulldog Cafés" where "soft" drugs can be bought.

All day tourist boats travel along Amsterdam's canals, which are crossed by some 400 bridges. The most beautiful houses line the Prinsengracht and Herengracht canals. The houses are very narrow, and their top floors jut out with a hook and pulley at the top to lift furniture which cannot be taken up the narrow stairs. The house **gables** are beautifully shaped.

Below *Some of the elegant houses on Prinsengracht, with hooks and pulleys on their gables.*

Left *Beautiful flowers can be bought at the flower market on Singel canal.*

Below *In the narrow streets of central Amsterdam the bicycle is the most convenient form of transportation.*

Famous landmarks in Amsterdam include the Royal Palace, the fifteenth-century Weeper's Tower, where it is said women wept as their husbands sailed for the **New World**, and the Begijnhof, a quiet square of charming **almshouses** surrounding the English Reformed Church.

There are more than 40 museums in Amsterdam. They include the Amsterdam Historic Museum, filled with paintings, furniture and costumes, and a magnificent Maritime Museum. Works of art are housed in the imposing Rijksmuseum, the Stedelijk and the Van Gogh Museum.

The cost of living in Amsterdam is generally lower than in other EEC capital cities, and living standards are therefore high. There is a busy night life and some bars and clubs stay open until dawn. On Sunday mornings, some people may just be making their way home as others are going off to church.

6 Towns and cities

Alkmaar, like many towns and cities in the Netherlands, is built on a network of canals.

The majority of Dutch people live in **urban** areas. Most Dutch towns began as small settlements on the waterways. These settlements gradually grew in size, often stretching along roads and railroads until they swallowed up other villages. Such built-up areas are called **conurbations**.

The largest conurbation, in the western Netherlands, is called Randstad (ring or edge town). When Randstad Holland was built it did not follow a plan. It simply grew up from many separate towns and villages which are linked together in a crescent shape. It has no center, and in between the towns there are still plenty of areas of countryside. The Randstad region includes Amsterdam, Utrecht, Haarlem, Lieden, The Hague, Delft, Rotterdam and Dordrecht.

In contrast, Flevoland, the newest province, which consists entirely of reclaimed land in the IJsselmeer, was carefully planned. Houses are built around the municipal capital of Lelystad. It is self-contained, with everything people need, and natural attractions and leisure parks have been built within a 30-minute drive. By the year 2000, Lelystad is expected to have a population of 100,000.

In the north of the country are the towns of Groningen and Leeuwarden. Like Amsterdam, and many other towns in the Netherlands, they have been built around a network of canals.

Above *The modern bus station in Lelystad, the newest city in the Netherlands.*

Below *Even highrise housing developments are built on the edge of water.*

7 Country life

Although flat, the Dutch countryside is very beautiful. **Barges** chug along canals, through meadows filled with browsing black-and-white cattle, and there are fields of green onions, red and yellow tulips, an occasional windmill, and rows of trees which seem to be leaning against the wind.

However, the Netherlands is becoming an increasingly urbanized country. Only about one-fifth of Dutch people live in **rural** communities and fewer than one in ten of the population work at farming, forestry or fishing. Many Dutch people feel that the spread of the towns into the countryside is spoiling its charm, but more and more businesses are moving out of towns to the country-side, looking for cheaper rents and quieter working conditions.

In the areas that are still rural, life is ruled by the seasons. Most people rise early, work hard and are asleep by 10:00 pm. Old customs are important to the Dutch, and traditional costumes are still worn by women in parts of Zeeland, Friesland and in the old ports along the shores of the IJsselmeer. Some farmers still prefer to wear wooden **clogs** rather than rubber boots.

Above Collecting reeds in Flevoland for making into cane furniture.

Right In rural areas women dressed in traditional costume can still be seen.

Right A farm on Marken, an island in the IJsselmeer linked to the mainland by a causeway.

Below Students often work during their vacations, harvesting onions.

Many of the permanent and part-time farm jobs are now filled by the Netherlands' immigrant population, and during the summer jobs are often taken by students, who can be seen digging tulip bulbs in North Holland or onions in Limburg.

The islands off the Dutch coast used to be quite isolated. Now some can be reached by dams and bridges. They are becoming popular with vacationers and tourists, and hotels, summer houses and camp sites are being developed.

8 Growing up

A weekday begins between 7:00 and 8:00 am, when children get up, feed their family pets and have breakfast. Most children ride their bicycles to school, although in bad weather they may take the bus, or be driven to school by one of their parents.

Birthdays are celebrated in a special way at school. When one of the class has a birthday, the pupil stands on a desk while the others sing *Hartelijk Gefeliciteerd* (Happy Birthday). The child then takes around cookies or little cakes for the teacher and classmates.

On long summer evenings, after they have done their homework, many children are allowed to play until about 9:00 pm. Many like to go fishing with friends.

Above *Children living in rural areas may go fishing after school.*

Below *Birthday cakes being passed around in class.*

On winter evenings, most children watch television for an hour or so before going to bed.

On a sunny weekend, most Dutch families go to the country, or to the beach. Roads are crowded with cars, many with bikes and windsurfers strapped on the back. Sometimes people take a picnic along. Other families put on their best clothes and visit Amsterdam, perhaps to go window-shopping, or to feed the pigeons in Dam Square, and have lunch in a restaurant. Returning home they may stop for afternoon tea with *poffertjes* (small pancakes and syrup) or *wafels met slagroom* (waffles and whipped cream).

Young Dutch children eat with their parents at around 7:00 pm. Dinner usually begins with soup, and favorite dishes are *kip* (chicken), pasta and grilled meat.

At vacation times, camping is popular, at the beach or at a woodland site. When children grow older, families go on automobile trips abroad, to countries such as Spain and France. By the time they are teenagers, most Dutch children are already familiar with other countries in the EEC.

Above These children, whose parents came to the Netherlands from the island of Sulawesi, in Indonesia, are playing outside their home.

Left Sometimes the whole family – grandparents, uncles, aunts and cousins – will all go out together for coffee and cakes.

9 Education

A geography lesson in a state-run elementary school.

For many years there has been equal government support for state schools and private denominational (religious) schools. Parents can choose the type of school they prefer, and over half of Dutch children attend private schools.

Lessons usually begin at 8:30 am and end at 3:00 pm, with a short lunch break. There are not more than 30 pupils in each class. Besides general subjects, arts and crafts and music are taught. Popular elementary school sports are soccer, table tennis, basketball and judo, and many schools also teach gymnastics. English classes are compulsory from the age of eleven, but many children have become used to hearing English by this time and will already be familiar with some words. A second foreign language, usually French or German, may be studied at the secondary level.

Above Although Dutch children do not start school until they are six years old, they may attend nursery school.

Children usually begin school at the age of six, although they may attend nursery school before that. When they are age twelve they move on to secondary school, where **vocational skills** are taught in addition to general subjects. After the age of sixteen, pupils may either leave school, specialize in vocational training, or stay on until eighteen and then go to a university.

The first university in the Netherlands was the University of Leiden, founded in 1575. It is still the leading university in medicine and law. Queen Beatrix (the present Queen of the Netherlands) is a law graduate of Leiden. There are thirteen universities, but since so many students want to enrol they are chosen by lot. Courses such as medicine and dentistry are the most popular.

Bicycles belonging to students, parked outside Amsterdam University.

The religious diversity throughout Dutch society and schools also extends to the universities. For example, the Free University of Amsterdam is based on Protestant **Calvinist** ideals, while the universities at Nijmegen and Tilberg are Roman Catholic.

10 Food and drink

Dutch food, although simple, is healthy and very filling. At breakfast people have fruit juice, tea or coffee, a cereal, and various breads (including crispbreads), with a boiled egg, cheese and cold meats. Children may put *hegelslaag* (chocolate or aniseed flavored spread) on their bread.

Left A typical Dutch breakfast includes boiled eggs, cheese and different kinds of bread.

Below Thick homemade soups are very popular.

Lunch is usually light, with salads, cold meats and cheese, of which there are more than thirty varieties. Two of the best-known are Edam and Gouda. Russian eggs (hard-boiled with diced potatoes and mayonnaise) is a popular lunch.

In the evenings, people usually dine before 8:00 pm. Soups are very popular, especially green-pea soup with onion and ham, and *groentensoep* made from vegetables, vermicelli and meatballs. Among the dishes that might be eaten for the main course are *boerenomelet* (an omelet stuffed with potato, meat and vegetables), *boerenkool met rookwurst* (a kale and potato dish eaten with mixed vegetables) and *klapstuk* or beef stew. Although fish is very expensive, it is much enjoyed and the mussel season is eagerly awaited.

Popular snacks include smoked eel, shrimp, herring and raw minced steak stuffed in soft bread rolls. Herring is also eaten raw or salted, with chopped onion. French fried potatoes with mayonnaise are a great favorite, and lines of people form outside the French fry stands. Other snacks are hot dogs, hamburgers, ice creams and *appelbeignets* (apple doughnuts).

Pannekoeken (pancakes) are a Dutch specialty. They are always large, and form a meal in themselves. There are lots of fillings to choose from, and they may be served with syrup, or with bacon.

Although traditional Dutch cooking

This Indonesian girl is eating a traditional Dutch delicacy – raw herring.

is quite plain, the Dutch love the spicy foods that have been introduced by the immigrant population. Chinese, Indonesian and Tunisian restaurants are among the most popular. A favorite meal is *rijstaffel*, consisting of rice with 20 to 30 different Indonesian dishes.

The most typical Dutch drinks are *genever* (Dutch gin), and *pils* (a light lager). Dutch Heineken beer is exported all over the world. Famous Dutch liqueurs are orange-flavored Curaçao, and Advocaat, which has raw eggs in it.

11 Shopping

Above Dutch cheeses being sold from a market stand in Amsterdam.

Right A selection of Dutch currency. The basic unit of currency is the guilder (or gulden), which is divided into 100 cents.

Busy weekly markets are a characteristic of the Netherlands. They sell everything from fresh farm produce and homemade cookies to embroidery and plants. Many towns have weekend "flea markets" selling second-hand goods. There are also specialized weekly markets such as the wholesale cheese market held every Friday morning in Alkmaar, where the porters wear the uniform of the 300-year-old Cheese Carrier's Guild. The world's largest **auction**,

at Aalsmeer, handles about 9 million flowers every weekday.

Besides buying in the weekly market, Dutch families stock up at supermarkets such as "Spar" and "Albert Heyn." Specialty food stores are a feature of the Randstad cities.

In the towns there are big department stores, such as the Dutch-owned C & A and "De Bijenkorf" in Amsterdam. There are also many art stores and antique shops in Amsterdam, and plenty of jewelry stores. Whatever the type of store, Dutch shopkeepers are always polite and helpful; they will gift wrap the smallest purchase as part of the service.

Above A pedestrian shopping area in Amsterdam where not even bicycles are allowed.

Left A Dutch supermarket. Kitchen utensils are hung on the shelves next to the food to tempt people to buy them.

12 Sports and leisure

The Dutch people make full use of their leisure time. Bicycling is a favorite pastime, and entire families, even tiny children, are to be seen bicycling along the dikes and through fields and woodland on weekends and during vacations whenever the weather is fine.

About a quarter of the Dutch population enjoys sports of some kind. With a million members, soccer clubs are the most active, and tennis and jogging are also popular.

The many lakes, canals and rivers offer plenty of opportunities for swimming, canoeing, fishing, windsurfing and sailing. Windsurfers brave all weathers on the open waters of the IJsselmeer and the Schelde estuary. Every waterside town has a marina filled with boats. Sailing conditions are ideal, not only for modern yachts, but also for traditional sailing barges or *skûtsjesilen*. Summer races are held between these colorful old vessels.

The lakes and estuaries of the Netherlands are ideal for windsurfing.

The Dutch also love fishing. Wherever there is water – a canal or a pond – someone is sure to be sitting in a chair holding a rod.

Marathon walking is another summer event, while skating is a traditional winter activity. As many as 17,000 people compete in long-distance skating races. When the IJsselmeer freezes, boats with runners sail across the ice.

Left *A traditional sailing barge racing a more modern yacht.*

Fishing is a very popular and relaxing pastime.

When the canals freeze over, people can travel for long distances on the ice.

On weekends, many people may visit the cities to go window-shopping and explore the flea markets. Shopping streets in Amsterdam and Rotterdam are crowded until late on a Saturday night.

Families spending their vacations at home visit local museums, exhibitions and parks. The miniature village of Madurodam, near The Hague, built to one twenty-fifth scale, attracts large crowds, and Flevohof, a park in Flevoland, with **punting**, gardens and games, has attractions for both young and old. The dazzling tulip displays in the Keukenhof Gardens in Lisse, South Holland, draw people from all over the Netherlands. Linneaushof, near Haarlem, is an amusement park with over 300 attractions for children.

About a third of the Dutch people spend their vacations outside the Netherlands. Spain, Greece, Tunisia and the Canary Islands are the most popular destinations. Some families may travel even farther afield to places such as Indonesia or the Netherlands Antilles, which used to be Dutch colonies.

Left *The miniature village of Madurodam includes copies of many famous buildings in the Netherlands. It commemorates a young man who died in World War II, and profits from it go to charities concerned with helping young people.*

Below *Scheveningen is a popular vacation resort on the coast, not far from The Hague.*

13 | Religion and festivals

Religion has played an important part in Dutch history and has both united and divided the Dutch nation. Since 1848 there has been complete religious freedom in the Netherlands. Most people are either Roman Catholic or Protestant, belonging to the Dutch Reformed Church. Nowhere in the EEC are there so many religious institutions: there are Catholic and Protestant schools and universities, newspapers and radio stations, social and sports clubs, hospitals and homes for the elderly.

Membership in the Church has gradually fallen during this century, although it is still an important part of daily life in rural areas. In some country towns, Catholic and Protestant neighbors are polite to each other but may never have visited each other's homes.

Many Dutch festivals have religious origins. The most important festival in Amsterdam is on December 5. On this day *Sinterklaas* (St. Nicholas), the patron saint of children, rides into Amsterdam on his white horse. The horse is led by his servant, Black Peter, whose job is to find out if all the children have been good. It is traditional for him to carry a bundle of sticks to punish any bad children. People stop work as St. Nicholas rides into **the Dam**, and the Lord Mayor of Amsterdam offers him a beaker of wine. Presents are

Sinterklaas (St. Nicholas) and his assistants arriving in Amsterdam to hand out presents to children on December 5.

then handed out to children of poor families.

On Christmas Eve, Catholics light the fifth candle on the *adventskraan*, a ring of woven pine-needles hung from the ceiling. Both Catholics and Protestants may attend a midnight or early morning service in their respective churches. On Christmas Day, relatives and friends may come to call bringing presents, and the Christmas dinner, with turkey or rabbit, is eaten around the family table in the evening.

At Easter it is the custom for children to search for eggs hidden by the "Easter Bunny." They also play a game called *Eiertikken*, which involves bumping the eggs together to see whose breaks first. On Ascension Day, a dawn visit, *Dauwtrappen* (treading the dew), is made to the countryside. The second Saturday in May is National Windmill Day, when windmills are set in motion. Flower festivals are popular, and public holidays are marked by floats, dancing, games and street stands.

Above Floats being decorated with hundreds of thousands of fresh flowers for a procession.

Right Crowds line the streets to watch a procession go by.

14 Culture and the arts

Above Delftware being painted in the Royal Factory.

Left A self-portrait by the artist Vincent Van Gogh, painted in 1888.

The Netherlands has been described as a living museum. The glorious period of seventeenth-century Dutch culture is still evident in many cities. There are more than 500 museums in the Netherlands. The famous Rijksmuseum in Amsterdam has paintings by Rembrandt, the greatest of the seventeenth-century Dutch school of artists. There have been many brilliant Dutch painters, and the museums are full of portraits, landscapes, and scenes from daily life. The Kroller Muller Museum near Arnhem has more than 1,500 paintings, including 300 by the nineteenth-century artist Van Gogh. There are other museums for special subjects such as stamps, streetcars, fishing and costumes.

The Netherlands is famous for its many crafts. One of the best-known craft products is porcelain from Delft. More than 30 different potteries made this "Delftware" in the seventeenth and eighteenth centuries, but now only the Royal Factory remains, where everything from tiles to vases is handmade. Other local products are pewterware and silver from Schoonhaven, goldware from Zeeland, candles, ceramics and handmade pipes from Gouda, and crystal from Leerdam and Maastricht. Popular tourist souvenirs are tiny blue-and-white china windmills, wooden clogs, costumed dolls and Dutch cheeses.

Inspired by this rich, cultural heritage, the arts of painting, sculpture, opera, theater, ballet and mime still flourish today. The Amsterdam Concertgebouw Orchestra, the Dutch National Ballet, and the Nederlands Dance Theater are all world famous and frequently perform abroad.

There are festivals of music of all kinds, including the annual North Sea Jazz Festival held in The Hague, which features artists from all over the world.

Left Although these days clogs are mainly used only when traditional costume is worn for special occasions, they are popular with tourists.

Below The modern concert hall and theater in The Hague.

15 Farming and fishing

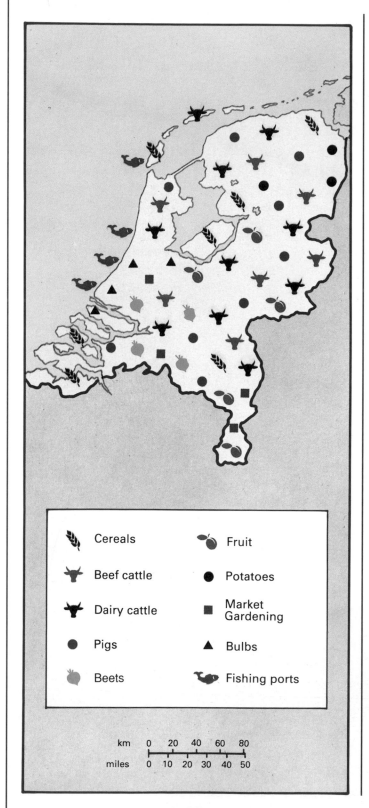

Legend:
- Cereals
- Beef cattle
- Dairy cattle
- Pigs
- Beets
- Fruit
- Potatoes
- Market Gardening
- Bulbs
- Fishing ports

km 0 20 40 60 80
miles 0 10 20 30 40 50

Conditions in the Netherlands are ideal for farming, especially on the fertile new polders in the IJsselmeer. Almost two-thirds of all farmland is pasture. Dairy farming takes place mainly in the wetter districts of the north and west, where the grassland is ideal for milk production. Improved breeding and feeding methods have increased the output to such an extent that the EEC has had to set limits on how much milk a farmer may produce. Intensive farming of livestock – calves (for veal), pigs and poultry – is also important.

Crops are grown near the coast and in Flevoland. They consist mainly of wheat and corn, beets, potatoes, onions and peas. The southern half of the country has many acres of market gardening and about one-tenth of this is under glass. Most vegetables, fruit and bulbs are grown outside, but lettuces, cucumbers, tomatoes and flowers are grown in greenhouses. The Netherlands exports cut flowers and bulbs all over the world and has been nicknamed the "Florist of Europe."

The Dutch fishing industry has declined in recent years. This is largely because overfishing in the North Sea and Irish Sea has resulted in poor catches. The EEC has now set limits on the catches of cod and herring in order to give the fish time to breed. Important fishing ports are Harlingen, in Friesland, and the old Zuider Zee towns. Elburg is one of the ports known for its smoked eels. In the southwest, shellfish "farming" is important and shrimp are caught offshore. Shellfish such as oysters and mussels are exported to other EEC countries.

Right Mussels being harvested on a shellfish farm in Zeeland.

Below Tulips being harvested and packed into wicker baskets.

16 Industry

Rotterdam, with its large port, is the industrial center of the Netherlands.

Industry in the Netherlands has coexisted with farming and fishing since the early days of the **Industrial Revolution**. The country has some natural resources of coal, oil, gas and salt, but most raw materials have to be imported.

While most towns have some factories, heavy industries are centered in Rotterdam. It is the world's biggest port and the largest town in the Netherlands. The transportation of goods to other EEC countries is a vital part of the Dutch economy. About one-third of all EEC goods pass through Dutch ports, in particular through Rotterdam's "Europoort." Here, the ECT (Europe's container load terminal) handles more than 1.5 millon containers every year.

Three of the world's biggest companies – Philips, Unilever and Shell – are Dutch. Amsterdam has become the most important diamond center in the world, and the skills of the Dutch at engineering, dredging, construction, shipbuilding and aircraft production are known worldwide.

Among the oldest manufacturing industries are food, drink, tobacco and textiles, although EEC agreements with outside companies have recently limited textile production and caused some unemployment. Manufacturing, especially of metal goods such as machines, automobiles, tools, furniture and household equipment, are now an important source of income. The electronics industry has also grown rapidly in recent years.

Since World War II (1939–45), tourism has become a major industry. Coastal resorts, the Frisian Islands, the towns and villages of the IJsselmeer and many fine historic towns and cities are popular tourist centers. Each year, in April and May, thousands of tourists travel from all over the world to see the bulb fields in bloom. There are special "bulb routes" signposted along the roads through the major bulb-growing areas, and the flower auctions at Aalsmeer have become one of the leading tourist attractions.

Left *Because of its long-standing connection with South Africa, a country rich in diamonds, the Netherlands has developed a thriving diamond cutting industry.*

Below *Tourism brings in millions of dollars every year, particularly at tulip time.*

17 Transportation

Wherever you are in the Netherlands you will always see bicycles and cyclists. About 11 million people own bicycles. They bike to work or to school, or for pleasure, along special bicycle tracks that have been built in the towns and cities and throughout the countryside.

The Netherlands is also famous for its huge network of waterways. More than 2,670 mi (4,300 km) are **navigable** and used for transporting people and freight. There are over 180,000 inland waterway barges carrying goods to and from other EEC countries.

Below Barges are one of the principal forms of transportation for industrial goods.

Rotterdam and Amsterdam are both important ports. Each year more than 30,000 seagoing vessels call at Rotterdam to load or unload freight. Ferry services run between England and the Dutch ports of Vlissingen (Flushing), Rotterdam and the Hook of Holland.

Below Car ferries allow automobiles and trucks to travel to the United Kingdom.

Above KLM planes at Schipol Airport near Amsterdam.

The 1,864-mi (3,000-km) electrified railroad network, carrying more than a billion passengers a year, is one of the most efficient in the world.

The Netherlands also has a good highway system and excellent public transportation. There is a ticket system that allows people to use the same ticket on buses, streetcars, and in the subway, in the course of one day.

Tunnels are vital to local transportation. Although bridges are still to be seen in many areas, tunnels have been built where road traffic is heavy. An important tunnel runs under the Maas River in Rotterdam. Another is the IJ tunnel for traffic out of Amsterdam.

Streetcars, like this one in Amsterdam, run through the streets on rails.

Schipol Airport, just south of Amsterdam, is Europe's fourth busiest airport. It is the base for KLM (Royal Dutch Airlines), which flies to 76 countries. Another airline, NLM, operates a "cityhopper" service between Schipol and the larger towns.

18 Government

Queen Beatrix with her husband, Prince Claus von Amsberg, and their three sons.

Upper House (the Senate) and a Lower House. The Upper House has 75 members who are elected by Provincial Councils. The Lower House has 150 members who are elected every four years. All Dutch people over the age of 18 may vote for them. Queen Beatrix, the Head of State, appoints the Cabinet Ministers. Although ministers are responsible to the parliament, every act or decree, besides having the signature of the minister responsible, must also have the signature of Queen Beatrix.

The Netherlands is a **constitutional monarchy**, which means that although it has a royal family, their powers are limited by Parliament. The present Dutch monarch, Queen Beatrix, is a descendant of William of Orange (1772–1844).

The Netherlands is divided into 12 provinces and 850 municipalities. The Houses of Parliament, or *Binnenhof*, are in The Hague. The name of the Dutch parliament is the States-General. It consists of an

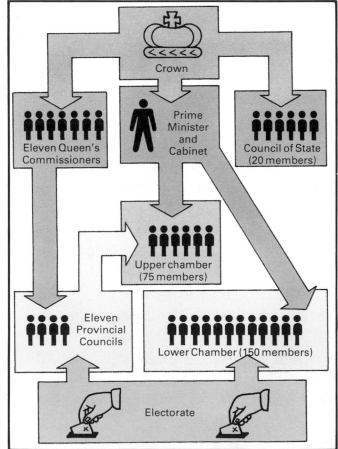

In the Netherlands, the government provides funds to help all people in need. Although the government does not provide housing, it does give loans and **grants** for people to buy new homes and to improve existing homes. All Dutch people may claim a family allowance for each child. At the age of 65, no matter what job they have or how well-off they are, everyone is entitled to claim a state pension.

Health care is paid for mainly through an insurance system. In return for regular contributions to a fund, people receive free medical, dental and hospital care, although people with a high income are required to take out private insurance. The health-care system works well. Improved working and living conditions, and excellent medical standards, mean that the average life expectancy is 72 years for men and 79 years for women. Non-government organizations, usually religious orders, care for those elderly people who need help.

The Dutch Houses of Parliament in The Hague are bordered by an ornamental lake.

19 Facing the future

The Netherlands has long had the reputation of being a peace-loving and tolerant nation with a strong belief in human rights. It was one of the first countries to grant freedom to slaves in the nineteenth century, and today representatives from countries all over the world come to settle disagreements at the International Court of Justice in The Hague.

However, Dutch tolerance also has brought some problems. The government's relaxed attitude towards the sale and use of **"soft" drugs**, for example, has resulted in the increase of illegal sales of **"hard" drugs**, and drug abuse is found, especially among the young unemployed in the larger cities.

Over the years the Netherlands has been a safe place for persecuted minorities, including in this century political and social **refugees**. The government has tried to promote measures to help the immigrant population fit into Dutch society, but although there are equal opportunities in education and housing, many immigrants speak little Dutch and can find employment only in low-paying jobs, such as agricultural work and cleaning. Most of them admit, however, that the Netherlands does offer them a chance to improve their living standards. When they are able to find work, most earn ten or twenty times more than their family or friends in their countries of origin.

Left The Bulldog Café in Amsterdam where "soft" drugs may be obtained.

Right The Dutch are leading the battle against the pollution of the North Sea which is affecting fish stocks, seals and sea birds.

Below People from countries all over the world find work and a home in the Netherlands.

Faced with the problems of floods, the Dutch have always been aware of the need to care for their environment. They are particularly concerned about the levels of chemical pollution in the Rhine River and the North Sea. In 1971, the Netherlands helped to draft an agreement banning the use of **biological weapons**. It has also declared its opposition to putting weapons in space.

Although the Netherlands is a small country, it is highly respected by the rest of the world. In the last thirty years, it has developed into one of the most forward-looking countries in Europe. The destruction of the war years (1939–45) and the independence of Indonesia in 1949 meant a loss of wealth to the Netherlands, but successful industrialization has rebuilt the economy.

Glossary

Almshouse An institution for the needy paid for by public or private funds.

Auction A public sale at which things are sold to the person who offers the highest price.

Barge A long, flat-bottomed boat, used for carrying goods on rivers and **canals**.

Biological weapons Weapons that use germs to kill plants, animals and humans.

Calvinist One who follows the religious teachings of John Calvin (1509–64).

Canal Channel dug to carry water.

Catholic A Christian who accepts the Pope as head of the Church.

Clogs Wooden shoes traditionally worn by Dutch people.

Colony A country taken over by a stronger country.

Constitutional monarchy A country ruled by a king or queen, whose power is limited by laws and a constitution.

Conurbation A large built-up area formed by the joining up of separate towns.

Delta project The series of dams and dikes which prevent flooding of the land at the mouths of the Rhine, Maas and Schelde rivers.

Dike A wall built to keep water from flooding the land behind it.

Estuary The widening channel of a river as it reaches, and mixes with, the sea.

European Economic Community (EEC) A trade association of twelve countries, which also has a Parliament and a Court of Justice. The member countries are: Belgium, France, West Germany, Italy, Luxembourg, the Netherlands (who were all founders in 1958), the United Kingdom, the Irish Republic and Denmark (joined 1973), Greece (1981), Spain and Portugal (1986).

Gable The triangular section of a wall enclosed by the end of a roof.

Grant Money given for a specific purpose.

"Hard" drugs Popular term for drugs, such as heroin, which are harmful and addictive.

Immigrant A person coming to live in a country from another country.

Industrial Revolution A period in the early nineteenth century when industry developed very quickly and many people left the countryside to work in towns and cities.

Lock A gate across a canal, which can be opened to let water and barges through.

Maritime Bordering on the sea. A term used to describe a country that uses the sea for transportation and fishing.

Navigable Wide, deep, or safe enough to be sailed on or through.

New World North and South America.

Polder Low-lying land reclaimed from water and protected by dikes.

Protestant A Christian who does not accept the Pope as head of the Church.

Punting Using a pole to propel a flat-bottomed boat.

Refugee A person who has to leave his or her country because of persecution, war or famine.

Resistance A secret organization fighting for the freedom of a country against an enemy occupying army.

Rural A term describing features of the countryside. The opposite of **urban**.

"Soft" drugs Popular term for drugs such as cannabis (marijuana).

The Dam A square in Amsterdam. It marks the place where the first barrier was built over the Amstel river in about 1270.

Urban A term describing features of towns and cities. The opposite of **rural**.

Vocational skill A skill which can be used to earn a living.

Windmill A machine for grinding or pumping, driven by wind which turns wooden "sails."

Books to read

Jacobsen, A. P., & Kristensen, Preben, *A Family in Holland* (Bookwright, 1984).
Kristensen, Preben, and Cameron, Fiona, *We Live in Belgium and Luxembourg* (Bookwright, 1986).

Kristensen, Preben, and Cameron, Fiona, *We Live in the Netherlands* (Bookwright, 1985).
Markl, Lise, *Living in Maritime Regions* (Franklin Watts, 1988).

Picture acknowledgments

All photographs were taken by Christine Osborne with the exception of the following: Aldus Archive 11; The Bridgeman Art Library 8, 9 (top), 10; E.T. Archive 9 (bottom); Chris Fairclough 7 (right), 27 (right), 33 (top), 40 (bottom); Netherlands Board of Tourism 30, 33 (bottom), 40 (top), 42; Topham 25, 32, 37 (bottom), 45 (top); Zefa: cover, 16 (Klaus Kerth), 21 (left), 31 (top) (Kotoh), 34 (right) (V. Phillips), 38, 39 (bottom) (Kotoh).

Index